BIG WORDS FOR LITTLE PEOPLE

Helen Mortimer & Cristina Trapanese

Kindness

OXFORD
UNIVERSITY PRESS

Welcome

It can start with a word.

When someone is new, it is kind to welcome them in and make them feel at home.

Sharing

Sitting together with a book is just one way to share.

If someone looks shy, why not try sharing a smile with them?

Giving

We all have the gift of giving.

But giving doesn't have
to be things you can see.

We can give encouragement
and comfort or we can even
give our time.

Understanding

Understanding how someone else might be feeling is important.

Especially if they're not having as much fun as you.

Listening

When we listen to others, we discover the things that matter to them.

Helping

When everyone
helps each other,
it makes our world
a kinder place.

Helping people can get them out of a pickle.

Thank you

Caring

Flowers need care
to grow and be happy.

Just like us.

Being thankful

We can be thankful for parties and
our friends and for rainbows
if it rains.

Loving

Reaching out
with warm words and kind
actions can show someone
that you love them.

It feels good to
be loved.

Taking turns

Waiting for your turn
can be difficult.

It is kinder to
be patient than
to push in front!

Thoughtful

Be as thoughtful as you can. Think about what your friends need, or what makes them happy.

Kindness

It can start with a word.

But sometimes we
don't have to say
anything at all.

Act kindly. Show kindness. Be kind.

Ten ideas for getting the most from this book

1   Take your time. Sharing a book gives you a precious chance to experience something together and provides so many things to talk about.

2   This book is all about what it means to be kind. Talk about kind actions and people that you have noticed around you today.

3   It's also a book about language. Ask each other what words you would use to describe being kind.

4   The illustrations in this book capture various moments at a party. We've intentionally not given the children names—so that you can choose your own and perhaps invent something about their personalities. What name would you give the dog?

Rex?
Banjo?
Kitten?
Boris?

5 Why not suggest what might have happened just before each moment and what might happen next?

6 Try to get inside the heads and hearts of each child. What is important to them?

7 Remember that sometimes there is distance between the words and the pictures. The words might be describing a way to be kind while the picture might show the opposite.

8 By exploring ways to recognize and express how kindness can have a positive impact on everything we do, we hope this book will give children and the adults in their lives the tools they need to make sense of themselves and the world around them.

9 Encourage imagination—if you were invited to this party, what games would you like to play and who would you make friends with?

10 You could each choose a favourite kindness word from the book—it will probably be different each time you share the story!

Glossary

comfort – when we make someone feel better when they are hurt or upset

encouragement – when we help someone feel brave enough to do something new

patient – if you are patient, you can wait without getting cross or bored

pickle – to be in a pickle is a saying which means that someone is finding it hard to do something

understanding – working out what something means or how it works